My First Book of

SHAPES

by Diane Stortz

Illustrated by
Jan Rice

A CIRCLE

IS
ROUND.

FIND
ALL THE
CIRCLES.

A SQUARE

IS THE SAME
ON
ALL FOUR SIDES.

FIND
ALL THE
SQUARES

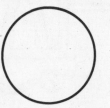

AND
CIRCLES.

A TRIANGLE

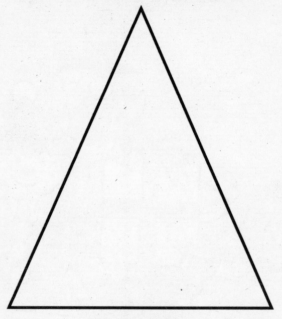

HAS
THREE SIDES.

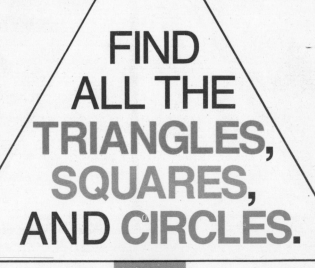

FIND
ALL THE
TRIANGLES,
SQUARES,
AND CIRCLES.

A RECTANGLE

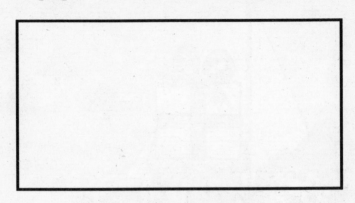

HAS TWO SHORT SIDES AND TWO LONG SIDES.

FIND
ALL THE
RECTANGLES,

TRIANGLES,

SQUARES,

AND CIRCLES.

A **DIAMOND**

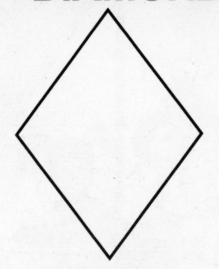

IS LIKE
TWO TRIANGLES
PUT TOGETHER.

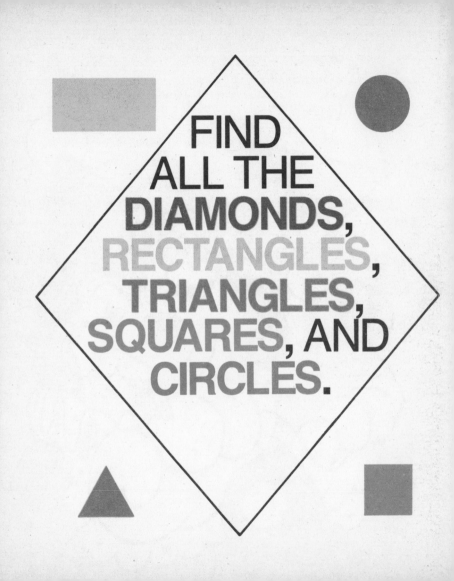

AN **OVAL**

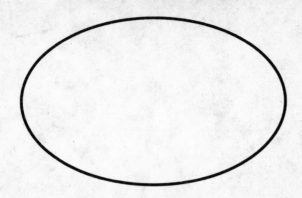

IS LIKE A STRETCHED-OUT CIRCLE.

FIND ALL THE
OVALS,
DIAMONDS,
RECTANGLES,
TRIANGLES,
SQUARES,
AND CIRCLES.